When it comes to jewelry, today's fashion pages, runway models and celebrities tell the same story: pendants. Chains and beaded strands don't just encircle the neck anymore; they dangle a distinctive stone or bead at the collarbone or drop a clustered tassel into the décolletage area.

Pendant necklaces are widely available in trendy shops, of course, but many savvy do-it-yourselfers have discovered the joys of making their own. You can create unique, one-of-a-kind necklaces to wear or give as gifts, or copy a piece you've admired on TV or in a magazine.

This book provides inspiration and instructions to help you make one or several chic necklaces, everything from collar-enhancing chokers to long, slim ropes. Whether hanging from metal wire, silk cording or beaded strands, exquisite pendants of all shapes and sizes are the featured stars here.

We've included a variety of styles and designs for necklaces to wear with elegant clothing or jeans and tees. Many are simple to make, with a few offering more challenge for the experienced jewelry maker. We also introduce you to the wonders of polyclay, with which you can create faux stones and beads or artistic baked-in designs.

Every material used in this book can be found at your local bead or craft store, and the projects can be made at a fraction of the cost of retail jewelry. Best of all, you'll have great fun creating beautiful accessories for all your clothing, as well as gifts for friends and relatives. Enjoy!

TABLE OF CONTENTS

EARTH, WIND AND FIRE

You'll need:

3 polished stone donuts in graduated sizes
2 terra-cotta bicone beads
2 terra-cotta tube beads
4 green and red multi-colored glass beads 10mm
1 spring crimp
24" black silk beading cord, 2mm

1. Stack the three donuts one on top of the other.

2. Fold the cord in half. Thread a loop through the holes of the donuts (A) and thread ends of the cord through the loop (B). Pull tight.

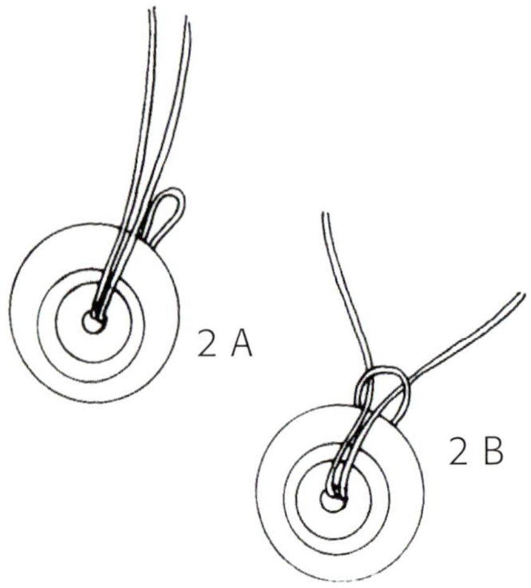

3. On one cord, measure 2" from donut and tie an overhand knot. Add one glass bead and one bicone bead. Measure up 2" and tie another knot. Add one glass bead and a terra-cotta tube bead.

4. Repeat this sequence on the opposite side.

5. Attach a spring crimp (see page 44).

Threading options

You don't have to use the traditional wire, threads and cords that are available for jewelry making. There are many other things that can be used to create truly original jewelry.

Hang an interesting pendant on a length of grosgrain ribbon for a choker.

Use silk ribbon for beading. It comes in luscious colors, knots nicely and is easy to work with.

Embroidery floss is another choice for making an interesting necklace. Available in hundreds of colors, this thread is strong, knots well and since it is 6-ply, can be separated and used as needed for the size of your beads.

Rattail cord – comes in two thicknesses and a wide variety of colors. It's a lovely shiny cord and works well when designing pendant necklaces.

A beautiful choker can be created with a length of decorative trim from the fabric store. Attach a charm pendant using a jump ring to the center front of the length of trim. Add a clasp and your choker is ready. How easy is that?

For a rustic, earthy looking necklace, twine or macrame cord can be used.

You'd be surprised what you can find in your local hardware store. You can purchase some very interesting chain by the yard to make a very unique necklace.

No artist can compete with Mother Nature, who always knows exactly how to combine her colors. The palette in a simple stone, a blissful blend of coppery tones, green and black, provides inspiration for this dreamy necklace. Similar shades are used to stack up a perfect pendant, with coordinating beads strung on silk cording.

CHARMING HEARTS

You'll need:
4 silver heart charms (various sizes)
3 green and 2 purple faceted beads, 12mm
5 greenish/purple faceted beads, 10mm
3 greenish/purple oval beads, 10x14mm
3 greenish/purple barrel beads, 6x8mm
160 lavender rocaille beads, 3mm
2 silver bead tips
2 silver jump rings
92″ nylon beading thread
Jewelry glue
Clasp

1. Cut two 36″ lengths and one 20″ length of thread.

2. Starting at the top of the bead board (see page 42), arrange your beads, starting with 3 rocaille beads.

Bead sequence for first strand

1 large bead, then alternate the faceted, oval and barrel beads as pictured.
9 rocaille beads

Repeat this sequence 5 times, then the same sequence for the opposite side. Thread these on to the 20″ length of thread.

3. For the drop and tassel: Thread one heart charm to the center of one 36″ length of thread and fold thread in half. Tie an overhand knot to secure in place. To form the tassel, thread the beads as follows: 3 rocailles, 1 small round faceted and 3 rocailles.

Repeat these instructions on the other 36″ length of thread with this sequence: first the heart charm, then 2 rocailles, oval faceted, 2 rocailles.

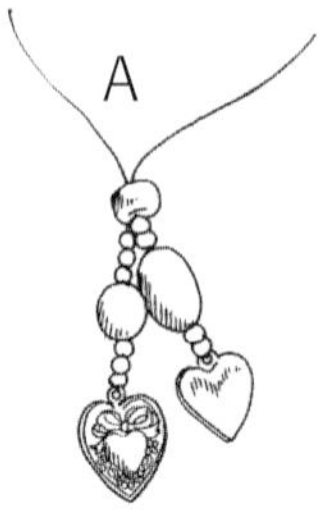

4. String both these tassels through the barrel bead and add 1 rocaille, then divide the thread. (see diagram A).

5. String each divided thread as follows: 9 rocailles, 1 round faceted, 9 rocailles, heart charm (with jump ring attached), 9 rocailles.

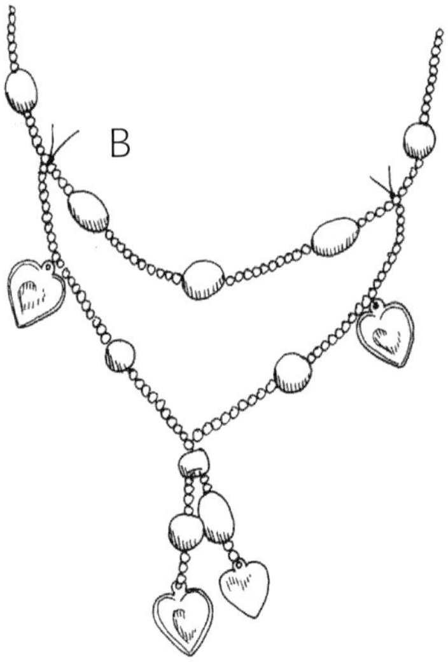

6. Tie each end of the drop to the first strand (see diagram B for placement). Add a dab of glue to the knot and trim excess thread.

7. Attach bead tips and clasp (see page 44).

The proud peacock boasts a breast of iridescent brilliance, a dazzling blend of colors that take the breath away. This hand-strung necklace celebrates this majestic color combination with rocaille and faceted beads accented with silver charms. The strands diverge and cross to create the look of a double pendant, the finale combining an eclectic assortment of beads and shiny hearts.

SOUTHWEST STYLE

You'll need:
Turquoise pendant with silver caps
29 rectangular turquoise beads
134 round assorted turquoise beads, 4mm and 6mm
14 flat turquoise beads
8 large turquoise beads, 10mm
12 medium turquoise beads, 8mm
8 silver double bead cups
14 round silver beads, 4mm
2 silver discs, 15mm
4 silver diamond shape beads
1 silver jump ring
6 silver crimp beads
3 strand clasp
72″ fine Flex Wire
Jewelry glue

1. Arrange the three strands of beads on a bead board using all three grooves.

Bead sequence for strand #1

2 - 4mm silver beads
1 rectangular turquoise
1 silver double bead cup
4 rectangular
Repeat 7 times, ending with 2–4mm silver beads

Bead sequence for strand #2

2 - 4mm silver beads
82 round turquoise beads (mix the 4mm and 6mm)
Continue until strand measures 18″
2 - 4mm silver beads

Bead sequence for strand #3

2 - 4mm silver beads
6 turquoise beads (mix the small, medium and flat)
1 silver diamond shape bead
12 turquoise beads (mixture)
1 - 15mm silver disc
12 turquoise beads (mixture)
1 - 4mm silver bead
Pendant with jump ring
1 - 4mm silver bead
Repeat the above sequence on the other side of the pendant.

2. Cut three lengths of wire – 22″, 24″ and 26″. When stringing beads, allow a 3″ tail on each end.

3. Start and end each strand with a 4mm silver bead.

4. When a strand is completed, attach a crimping bead on each end next to the silver bead.

5. String another silver bead on the wire and thread through the hole on the clasp. Tie an overhand knot and thread back through the silver bead. Dab glue and trim wire.

6. Repeat step 5 on each end. Match each strand to the same hole on the opposite clasp.

Here's a gleaming, teardrop pendant sure to set a turquoise-lover's heart afire. In textured silver and turquoise, it easily holds its own among a three-strand cache of beautiful, semi-precious baubles. Almost 200 cubes, nuggets, beads and discs of turquoise in varying hues are here, along with assortment of silver beads and spacers for perfectly placed shine.

TRUE BLUE

You'll need:
1 blue glass ½" bead
6 blue glass triangle beads
4 blue glass tube beads
4 blue glass bicone beads
2 silver spacer beads
1 silver eye pin, 2"
14 silver eye pins, 1"
Decorative silver bead cap
16 silver jump rings
24" silver chain with clasp
20 gauge silver wire
Wire cutters, needlenose pliers, and round nose pliers

1. To make the pendant: Cut a 7" length of 20 gauge wire and form a reverse spiral (diagram A). Thread a silver spacer bead on a 2" silver eye pin. Add a blue bead with a silver bead cap and another spacer bead (see photo). Form a loop at the top of the eye pin using round nose pliers. Trim the eye pin if necessary before forming a loop. Attach this loop to the bottom of the wire spiral using a jump ring and needlenose pliers.

A

2. To make the necklace: Lay the 24" chain on the bead board or flat surface. Position the pendant at the center of the chain.

3. Thread the blue triangle bead on a 1" silver eye pin. Add a silver spacer bead and form a loop at the top using round nose pliers. Again, trim the eye pin if necessary. Repeat these steps for each triangle bead.

4. Thread each tube bead and bicone bead on separate 1" eye pins and form a loop at the top of each.

5. Position beads around the chain as pictured. Attach the pendant and beads to the chain using silver jump rings.

About beads

Bugle beads – small glass tube bead that comes in a huge variety of colors and lengths.

Rocailles – tiny glass beads that are cushion shaped. They're available in vast array of colors and finishes. They're indispensable in jewelry designing.

Glass beads – these are also available in a myriad of colors, sizes and shapes. Most glass beads are handmade and will vary in size and pattern.

Metal beads – these can be gold, silver, copper or bronze and are available in many different sizes and shapes and come from all parts of the world. They're particularly useful when creating ethnic style jewelry, but can also be incorporated in classic, stylish jewelry.

Natural beads – these can be from such sources as shells, wood, seeds, and bone.

Plastic and resin beads – there are endless varieties of these man-made beads. They are the least expensive and most widely available.

Spacer beads - small metal beads used to decorate and separate other beads. Some are called "daisy" spacers.

This is a necklace an artist might wear, one who appreciates shape and substance, as well as the joys of uncluttered space. The placement celebrates the eclectic individuality of each of these glass beads, delighting the eye with interplay of deep cobalt blue and metallic silver. The unique pendant continues the love affair with shape and simplicity: a single spectacular bead, accented with silver dangles from a double spiral wire.

MIDNIGHT DELIGHT

You'll need:
2 polished stone donuts (1 large and 1 small)
3 yds black silk beading cord, 2mm
Jewelry glue

1. Place the smaller donut on top of the larger one and glue them together using the jewelry glue.

2. Cut three 36" lengths of cord.

3. Holding all three lengths together, fold the cords in half.

4. Thread the loop ends of the cords through the hole in the donut. Thread ends of the cord through the loop and pull up tight (see diagram).

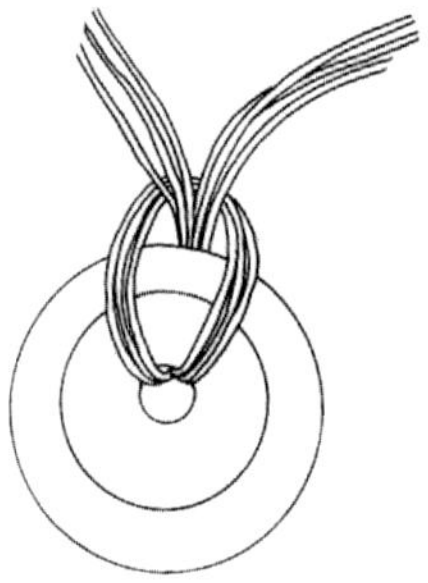

5. Tie a square knot (see page 45) in the ends of the cord to the desired length.

Alternative pendant ideas

We have used many different types of pendants in this book, but there are many others that could also be used. Keep your eyes open for objects that can be used as pendants in your own creative jewelry designs.

Shells
Vintage brooches
Coins
Pieces of broken china
Buttons
Native American silver pieces
Tear drop pearl
Filligree piece
Large African trade beads
Carved wooden piece

Each of nature's stones has a sediment-al story to tell. No two are alike, their individual characteristics emerging when weathered surfaces are polished to smooth perfection. Strung upon clustered strands of silk cording, a pendant of two layered stones creates a necklace of striking simplicity…uncomplicated beauty.

IVORY & EBONY

You'll need:
1 black-and-white inlaid bead, 1"
1 black-and-white inlaid bead, ½"
36 black metallic round beads, 5mm
18 silver metallic round beads, 5mm
2 round silver beads, 4mm
17 silver faceted beads, 6x8mm
1 small silver daisy spacer
22" Soft Flex wire
1 silver eye pin
2 bead tips
clasp

1. To form the pendant: Thread a 4mm silver bead, 1" black-and-white inlaid bead, silver daisy spacer, ½" black-and-white inlaid bead and one 4mm silver bead on eye pin. Using round nose pliers, form a loop at the top.

2. For the necklace: starting at the top of the bead board, arrange beads.

Bead sequence

1 - 5mm black metallic round
1 - 5mm silver metallic round
1 - 5mm black metallic round
1 - 6x8mm silver faceted bead

3. Repeat this sequence 9 times, then position the pendant on the board.

4. Again, starting at the top of the bead board, repeat this sequence on the opposite side.

5. To string the necklace: cut the wire and attach a bead tip to one end (see page 44). String beads onto the wire in the arranged order. When stringing is complete, attach a bead tip to the other end and add clasp.

Tip

Don't throw old necklaces away. You can always take them apart and use the beads in a new and different way.

It's fun to search through old jewelry at garage sales or flea markets to find special pieces that you can re-thread later.

Take apart these old treasures and separate the beads by sizes and color. Keep them in Zip lock bags and when you're ready to design a new piece – take out these bags and find just the perfect beads to combine and coordinate with others.

Keep another bag to collect and save findings from old necklaces and bracelets. These can really come in handy for future projects and will save you money, too.

Ebony and ivory are a classic color combination, as each bead in this pendant proudly attests. Both beads are daintily inlaid, and together, this striking twosome makes a bold graphic statement. Their ornamental clout is further enhanced by a choker of metallic black and silver beads. This is the necessary accessory for that little black dress.

BLUE LAGOON

You'll need:
7 blue/green glass beads, barrel shape
8 blue/green glass beads, cube shape
8 blue/green glass beads,
round shape, 10mm
10 blue/green glass beads,
round shape, 8mm
90 blue rocaille beads, 3mm
90 green rocaille beads, 3mm
66 gold metal round beads, 4mm
84" gold wire, 34 gauge
2 bead tips
Clasp
Jewelry glue

1. To make the tassel: Cut four 21" lengths of wire. Thread 1 gold metal bead on the wire leaving a 1" tail. Bring wire back around and thread through the bead again. Repeat this step on each piece of wire before threading the remaining beads. Dab ends of beads with glue and trim off excess wire.

2. Refer to the photograph for bead placement on each wire of the tassel.

3. When completed, thread all four wires through another gold bead, one 10mm round glass bead and one gold bead.

4. For the necklace: Starting at the top of the bead board, arrange beads.

Bead sequence

1 gold bead
5 rocaille beads (blue, green, blue, green, blue)
1 large blue/green bead (alternate shapes as pictured in photograph)

5. Repeat this sequence 3 times, then lay this same bead sequence on the opposite side of the board.

6. To thread the necklace, divide the wires of the tassel into two wires, and string the beads from the center "0" of the board in the sequence suggested.

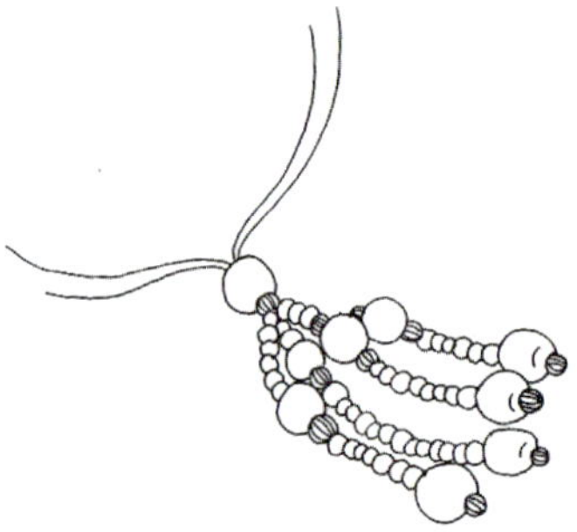

7. Attach bead tips and clasp to the ends of each wire (see page 44).

Let the splendor of this translucent, bead-cascade wash over you like a tropical waterfall in an azure sea. How it glints, dripping with cool glass and rocaille beads interspersed with tiny droplets of sunlit gold. The fluid bead pattern is a peaceful prelude to a bubbly finish–a four-strand tassel pendant that can't help but make a splash.

FROM THE SEA

You'll need:
Lavender abalone pendant
2 lavender frosted beads, 6x15mm
2 lavender frosted tube beads, 8mm
2 lavender round beads, 6mm
4 lavender bicone beads, 8mm
2 silver rocaille beads, 4mm
152 assorted rocaille beads, 3mm
48" beading thread (nylon or woven polyester), .04mm
2 bead tips
1 clasp

1. Arrange bead sequence on a bead board starting at the top.

Bead sequence

1 silver rocaille, 3mm
15 assorted rocaille beads, 3mm
1 frosted lavender bead (alternate sizes and types referring to photo)
2 rocaille beads, 3mm

2. Repeat this sequence 5 times on one side with the pendant in the center. Then repeat the bead sequence starting at the top of the other side of the board.

3. To string the necklace, cut the thread in two 24" lengths. Thread one piece through one hole in the pendant. Put both ends of the thread together and starting from the center, string beads on thread.

4. Repeat this sequence on the second length of thread.

5. When stringing is complete, add bead tips to each end (see page 44) and attach clasp.

Tip

When stringing beads and you can't find your needle, use a dab of glue on the ends of your beading thread. When dry, the thread will be stiff and beads will easily slide onto the thread – even without a needle!

You'll always find a swirling meld of sheer, tone-on-tone color in shells, a true gift of the sea. This one from the abalone, is heady with rich purple, an ideal color to celebrate in all its grand, varying shades. Beads of heather, plum and mauve share the spotlight with sheer crystal to create joyous strands for this lovely pendant. Tiny rocaille and glass beads are mixed with intriguing shapes of frosted resin to play up its unique shape.

EGYPTIAN FINERY

You'll need:
Jade donut
Egyptian tube bead, 1"
14 black faceted round beads, 8mm
21 black faceted round beads, 6mm
13 black faceted bicone beads, 4mm
6 jade round beads, 5mm
2 gold metal beads, 1"
7 gold metal round beads, 12mm
2 gold metal round beads, 4mm
8 large gold metal spacers
1 small gold metal spacer
30" beading wire, 20 gauge
2 end tips
Clasp

1. To form the pendant: fold the beading wire in half. Thread the loop end of the wire through the hole of the donut and bring up to the top.

2. Thread the two ends of wire through the loop and pull until the wire lays flat against the donut (see page 4).

3. String both ends of the wire through one 12 mm gold bead, the Egyptian bead and spacer. Pull beads down to meet the donut.

4. For necklace: Arrange beads on bead board.

Bead sequence

3 beads (either all black or black-jade-black)
Gold bead (alternate sizes and types)

5. Repeat this sequence eight more times on each side of the board.

6. Separate the two pendant wires. Position the pendant at the center of the arrangement and string each side starting at the center.

7. When stringing is complete, attach bead tips on both ends of wire and attach clasp (see page 44).

The legendary Cleopatra knew the power of beauty, and even she would be riveted by this gleaming temptation. This enticing necklace is highlighted by polished jade, with golden metals and raven-black faceted beads glimmering nearby. Set off by an Egyptian-style hieroglyphic bead, the satiny jade pendant beguiles, and your glamorous reputation is set in stone.

ASIAN IMPRESSION

You'll need:
Jade Pendant
3 carved wooden beads, ½″
Jade bicone bead, 8mm
18″ gold wire, 24 gauge
3 large gold jump rings
28″ black silk cord, 1mm
1 spring crimp
Jewelry glue

1. Cut three 6″ lengths of wire. Form a spiral on one end of each length of wire (see photo).

2. Thread the other end of the wire through one of the wooden beads and form a loop at the top. Trim the wire if necessary before making the loop. Repeat this step on the second wire. On the third wire, add the wooden bead with a jade bead on top, then form the loop.

3. Attach the wired beads to the pendant using jump rings.

4. Cut two 14″ lengths of the black cord. Attach one cord to each side of the pendant using a square knot (see page 45). Trim excess cord close to knot and apply a dab of glue.

5. Finish each end of the cord by attaching a spring crimp.

Tip

When you use cord that comes wrapped on a card, it will probably have bends or kinks in it. These can spoil the look of your finished piece. To remove these kinks, hang the necklace on a hook and let gravity do its job and the cord will straighten itself out.

Eastern philosophy says those who speak softly leave a lasting impression. A simple knotted silk cord secures an intriguing, tranquil pendant of Chinese jade, the carved, circular pattern echoing in a trio of wooden beads below. Spiraling pins and a matching bead add to an aura of mystery and finish the necklace, which seems to whisper of ancient oriental secrets.

FAR EAST PENDANT

You'll need:
Chinese pendant
225 coral rocailles, 2mm
225 silver lined rocailles, 2mm
225 iridescent rocailles, 2mm
3 silver beads, 3mm
3 silver eye pins, 2″
Bead clasp
Silver bail
78″ Power Pro braided bead thread, .006mm
Jewelry glue
6 crimp beads
2 silver end caps
Clasp

1. Cut three 26″ lengths of thread.

2. Leaving a 3″ tail on one end, attach a crimp bead (see page 44).

3. String all coral rocailles on the thread until the length measures 20″. Attach another crimp bead.

4. Repeat steps 2 and 3, stringing silver rocailles on the second thread, then the iridescent rocailles on the third.

5. Once all three strands are completed, tie them together at one end with an overhand knot and dab with glue.

6. Secure the tied end to a flat surface with tape and braid the strands together. When completed, tie together with an overhand knot.

7. Cut the head off of the eye pin using wire cutters. Form a loop to catch the knotted threads, then close.

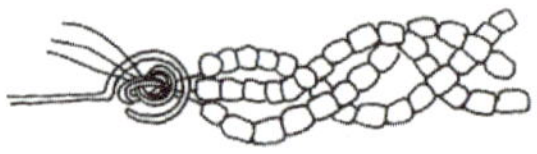

8. Thread an end cap over the eye pin so it covers the knot and loop. Trim the eye pin, but leave enough to form a small loop to attach the clasp.

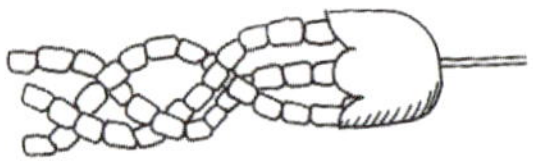

9. Repeat steps 7 and 8 on the opposite end of the necklace.

10. Attach a clasp to each end.

11. Thread silver bead, then pendant bead onto the eye pin. Form a loop on the other end and attach the bail to the loop, then close.

12. Thread the necklace through the bail.

Like tiny glistening raindrops in a springtime shower, streaming rocaille beads tumble and twist in a downward dance. The entwined, triplet strands echo the soft colors found in the radiant pendant that dangles from a silvery clasp. The pendant is delicately carved in an intricate pattern and speckled with tones of coral and flint.

GOLDEN HARVEST

You'll need:
Polished stone donut
52 rocaille beads, assorted colors, 3mm
4 gold metal beads, 4mm
2 multi-colored glass beads, 8mm
1 amber-colored glass bead, 8mm
12″ nylon beading thread
32″ black silk beading cord, 1mm
2 spring crimps
Jewelry glue

1. Fold the black cord in half. Thread a loop through the hole in the donut. Thread the ends of the cord through the loop and pull tight (see page 4). Add the amber glass bead.

2. Arrange the beads on the board.

Bead sequence

1 gold metal bead
1 multi-colored glass bead
1 gold metal bead
52 assorted rocaille beads
1 gold metal bead
1 multi-colored glass bead
1 gold metal bead

3. Thread the gold metal bead on beading thread leaving a 1″ tail. Bring the thread back around and thread through the bead again.

4. Thread the rest of the beads in the suggested sequence. End by bringing the thread back around the gold bead as before and threading it through again.

5. Add a dab of glue on each end and trim thread.

6. When the glue has dried, fold the string of beads in half. Thread the loop end through the donut and then thread the ends through the loop. Pull gently.

7. Place a dab of glue where the loop crosses over the threaded beads.

8. Use a square knot to tie the ends (see page 45).

Tip

To make a pendant from a cut stone shape, add the shape to an eye pin. Use the wrap loop to create a loop at the top. Add the pendant to your beaded necklace or a chain.

From sunrise to sunset, the burnished tints of this pendant will light up your eyes and keep you shining all day. Assorted beads encircle and frolic playfully to set off a fiery donut, mimicking its inspiring, golden hues. Glass and amber beads with metallic accents complete this ode to glowing, autumny color.

AFRICAN SAFARI

You'll need:
Round green turbo pendant
24 gold metal round beads, 4mm
2 amber glass beads, 8mm
4 amber glass beads, 10mm
2 amber glass beads, 4x18mm
2 amber glass beads, 8x12mm
36 iridescent tiger stripe bicone beads, 6mm
22″ fine Soft Flex wire
6″ gold wire, 24 gauge

1. To make the pendant: thread gold wire through the hole in the pendant and make a wrap loop (see page 45).

2. Arrange beads and pendant on the bead board.

Bead sequence

1 gold bead
3 bicone beads
1 gold bead
1 amber bead (varying sizes and types)

3. Repeat this sequence 5 more times alternating the amber beads (refer to photo). Add pendant.

4. Starting at the top of the board, repeat this pattern on the other side of the pendant, eliminating the last gold bead (see photo).

5. String the beads and pendant on the wire in the same order as on the board.

6. After stringing is complete, attach bead tip to the end and add clasp (see page 44).

Semi-Precious Stones

You can use semi-precious stones either as pendants or beads to create lovely necklaces. A beautiful slice of agate can make an interesting focal point as a pendant.

Some more common semi-precious stones are lapis lazuli, malachite, tiger eye, garnet, amethyst and turquoise.

These stones are not as expensive as you might think. Many are even cheaper than man-made beads.

You can combine semi-precious stones with metal beads, glass beads and other interesting baubles to come up with some really creative and special jewelry.

In rich, warm tones of yellow-green, gold and amber, this necklace smolders like a grassy African savannah at dusk. The glowing orb-shaped pendant is flecked with burnished, coppery tinges along with mossy green. Glass beads in round and bicone shapes are set off with golden spacers, creating a pleasing pattern of magnificent color.

CRYSTAL LEAVES

You'll need:
3 crystal leaves
5 gold metal beads, 10mm
10 black rocaille beads, 3mm
3 black and white bicone beads, 5mm
1 black oval disc, ½″
3 black bugle beads, 15mm
6 gold bugle beads, #3
1 gold eye pin, 1″
12″ nylon beading cord
24″ leather like cord, 1mm
1 spring crimp

1. For tassel pendant: Cut nylon cord into three 4″ lengths. Thread each cord through holes in the three crystal leaves.

2. Then thread each strand approximately as follows (we varied this sequence slightly).

Tassel bead sequence
1 black rocaille
1 black bugle bead
1 black rocaille
1 gold bugle
1 black bicone
1 gold bugle
1 black bicone

3. Thread all three strands through the oval disc bead and the loop of the eye pin. Pull the thread through until beads meet the oval bead and then tie securely to the eye pin. Trim excess cord.

4. Thread the eye pin through a gold bead. Using needlenose pliers, squeeze the loop of the eye pin so it will fit through the bottom hole of the bead so that the black oval disc and gold bead are touching.

5. Add black rocaille bead to the pin and form a small loop on the top. Trim excess wire if necessary before forming loop.

6. String the tassel pendant on the black cord and center it. Tie an overhand knot (see page 45) on each side of the pendant to hold it in place.

7. Starting at the center, measure up 2″ and tie another overhand knot. String a gold bead and again tie an overhand knot next to the bead. Space another bead 2″ from the first and repeat the knotting steps.

8. Repeat this sequence on the other side of the pendant.

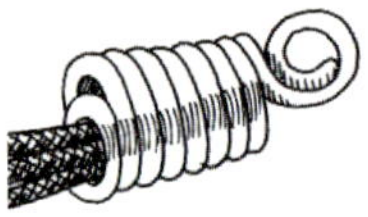

9. Attach a spring crimp and hook and squeeze the last coil (see page 44).

Depending on the design, a mix of gold and black can be elegant, authoritative, even bewitching! Here, a spartan length of leather-like cord is undisturbed but by a few gold-metal beads, until a tasseled pendant picks up the momentum. Emerging from beneath an inky disc is a three-pronged spray of tiny gold and black beads. They culminate in a surprising, grand finale: three gleaming, crystal-clear leaves.

TIGER'S EYE

You'll need:
Oval pendant of banana bark
6 faux agate disc beads, 16mm
18 round tiger eye beads, 6mm
6 round amber-colored beads, 10mm
6 amber-colored faceted tube beads, 1"
34 gold daisy spacer beads
24" fine Soft Flex wire
1 French hook earring finding
2 bead tips
Clasp

1. To make the pendant: cut off the "hook" end of the earring finding using wire cutters. Leave enough wire to thread through the hole in the pendant and form a hook wrap (A). The loop at the top of the finding will be used to thread the pendant on the wire.

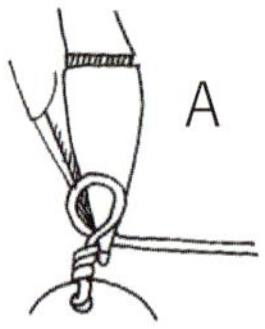
A

2. Starting at the top of the bead board, arrange the beads and pendant.

Bead sequence
1 gold spacer
1 - 10mm amber
1 gold spacer
1 - 6mm tiger eye
1 gold spacer
1 tube bead
1 gold spacer
1 - 6mm tiger eye
1 gold spacer
1 disc bead
1 gold spacer
1 - 6mm tiger eye

3. Repeat this sequence two more times. Add pendant.

4. Arrange the beads in this same sequence on the other side of the pendant, starting at the top of the bead board.

5. Cut the 24" length of wire and attach a bead tip to one end following instructions on page 44.

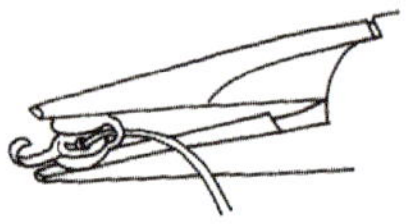

6. String the beads and pendant in the same arrangement as on the bead board.

7. When threading is complete, attach a bead tip to the other end and add the clasp.

Perfect for a day's prowl through the mall or a night on the town, this necklace is inspired by the beauty of the jungle-dwelling wildcat. The pendant shines like a glossy, spotted coat, while the glint in a tiger's eye is captured in beads of the same description. Amber tubes, agate discs, and glass beads are other tawny-colored accents set off by gold-toned spacers.

HEARTS AGLOW

You'll need:
Purple crackled abalone heart pendant
Decorative eye pin
60 glass faceted bicone beads, 4mm
14 lavender glass beads, 4x6mm
2 silver metal beads, 4mm
16 silver daisy spacers
2 bead tips (clam shells)
Clasp
22″ fine Soft Flex wire

1. To form the pendant: use round nose pliers to attach the decorative eye pin to the heart by threading the bottom of the pin through the hole in the pendant with the loop of pin at the top.
Bend the bottom of the eye pin up to meet the loop and wrap twice around the base.

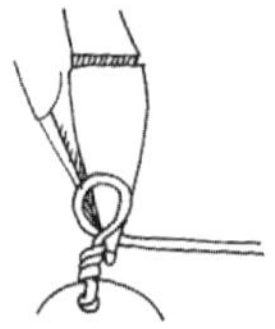

2. Arrange the beads starting at the top of one side of the bead board.

Bead Sequence
Silver daisy spacer
5 bicone beads
Silver daisy spacer
Lavender bead

3. Repeat this sequence five more times on one side.

4. Then, add one lavender bead, one spacer and the pendant.

5. Repeat the above on the other side of the board, again starting at the top.

6. Cut the 22″ length of wire and add a 4mm silver bead, then attach a bead tip to one end (see page 44). Thread the beads from the board, ending with a 4mm silver bead and bead tip on the other end. Add clasp of your choice.

A heart of gold is always an asset, but this pendant is an iridescent treasure. Your pulse will quicken each time the kaleidoscope of color is revealed by a beam of light–radiant hues of lavender, moss, shimmery white and more. Rich mother-of-pearl forms the pendant, held by sparkling strands of multi-dimensional glass and crystal beads and silvery spacers.

MOKUME GANE PENDANT

For polymer clay pendant you'll need:
Clay – 2 oz blocks of Black, Ultramarine Blue, Light Blue Pearl, Translucent, Purple (Premo!)
Silver leaf
Cutting template, Polyform Shapelets
Craft knife
Blade
Sculpey glaze, gloss
Needle tool
Wooden skewer

For necklace you'll need:
19 silver bugle beads, 1"
2 lavender glass beads, 8mm
12 silver beads, assorted
5-6 Lt. Blue Pearl clay tube beads
4 Ultramarine Blue clay tube beads
5 Purple clay tube beads
9 – 10 rocaille beads, assorted colors
3 silver spacers
Clasp
50" fine Flex Wire

To make the pendant:

See page 47 for mokume gane instructions.

1. Using a template, cut out two pendant shapes from a sheet of black clay with a craft knife.

2. Place the two shapes together with a wooden skewer sandwiched in between.

3. Roll out solid colors of Lt. Blue Pearl, Ultramarine Blue and Purple into skinny rolls. Slice the rolls into small beads. Pierce holes in each bead using the needle tool.

4. Place the pendant and beads on a parchment-covered baking sheet and bake in a 275° preheated oven for 20 minutes.

5. Remove all beads and pendant and let cool. Remove the skewer from the pendant.

6. When the pendant is cool, cover it with slices of the mokume gane, overlapping and covering the pendant front and back. Smooth down the clay with your fingers. Bake this piece in the oven for 20 minutes more.

7. Brush all the beads and pendant using glaze and let dry.

To string the necklace:

1. Lay out the beads on the board.

Approximate bead sequence
1 polymer clay bead
1 bugle bead
1 silver bead

2. Repeat this sequence 8 times alternating the colors of clay beads and a variety of silver beads.

3. End with one lavender glass bead and silver bead and the pendant.

4. Repeat the bead sequence on the other side of the board ending with the lavender glass bead.

For tassel:

1. Cut three 16" lengths of thread. String each one with a random selection of clay, rocaille and silver spacers and a silver bugle bead (refer to photo).

2. Put the three lengths together and thread on a silver bead, the pendant and another silver bead.

3. Divide the three lengths of thread into two lengths (two on one side, one on the other). Continue threading beads from the arrangement on your board, first on the left side and then on the right.

4. End with a clasp of your choice.

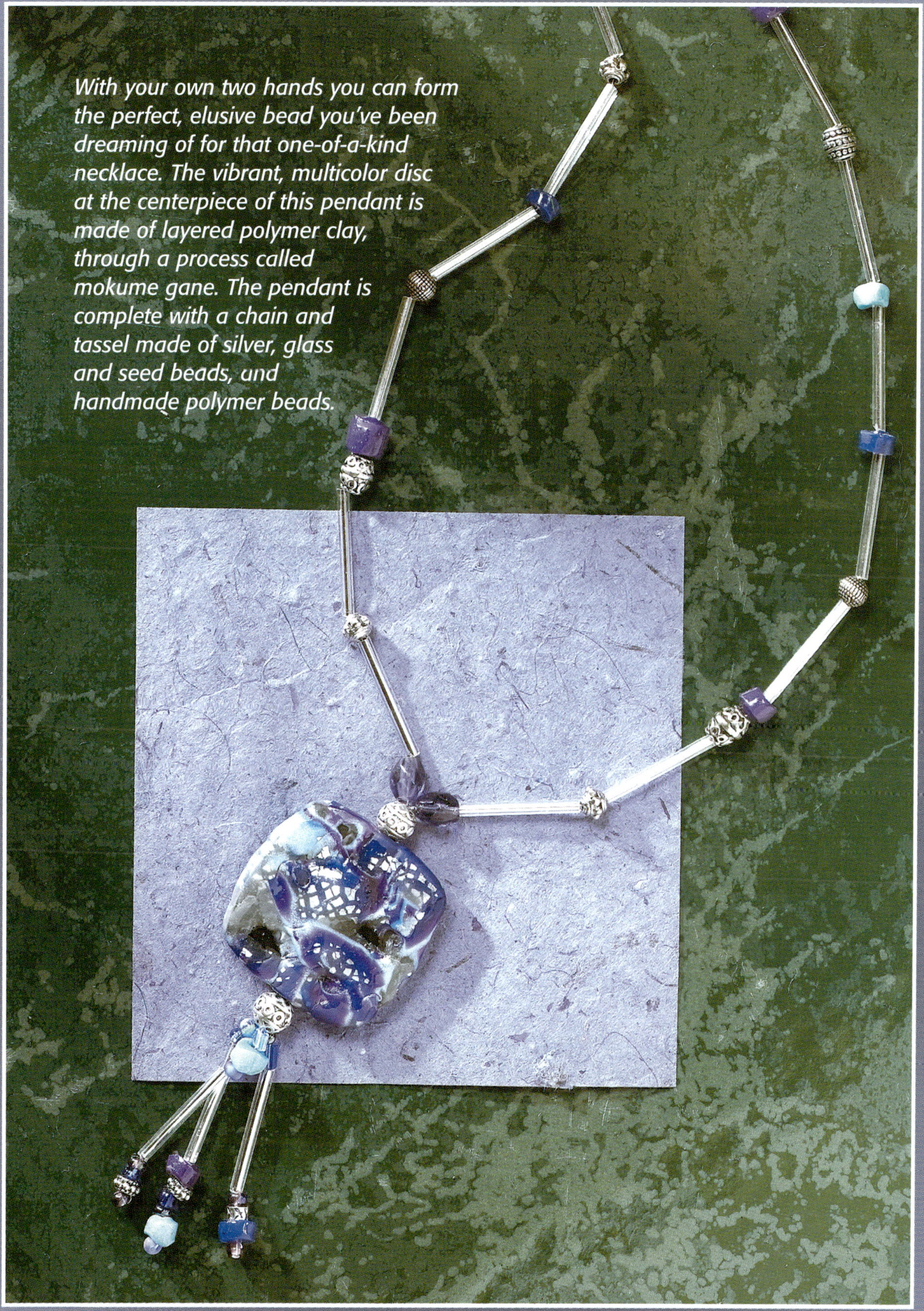

With your own two hands you can form the perfect, elusive bead you've been dreaming of for that one-of-a-kind necklace. The vibrant, multicolor disc at the centerpiece of this pendant is made of layered polymer clay, through a process called mokume gane. The pendant is complete with a chain and tassel made of silver, glass and seed beads, and handmade polymer beads.

DRAGONFLY

You'll need:
Clay: 1/4 block of Black, and Gold
Metallic powder: Spring Green, Misty Lavender, True Blue, Blue/Green (Pearl Ex)
Craft knife
Needle tool or wooden skewer
Small paintbrush
1 yd. turquoise waxed beading cord, 1mm
1 yd. purple waxed beading cord, 1mm
1 yd. dark blue waxed beading cord, 1mm
2 blue glass beads, 8mm
1 spring crimp

1. For the polymer clay pendant: Condition the black and gold clay (see page 46).

2. Roll the clay through the pasta machine on the thickest setting to form sheets of clay.

3. Press the dragonfly stamp into the black clay.

4. Using a craft knife, cut around the shape (referring to photo) leaving 3/4" at the top of the design.

5. Use a small paintbrush to blend the powdered colors onto the design.

6. Place the cut-out dragonfly piece on the sheet of gold clay and cut around it leaving about an 1/8" border.

7. Using your needle tool or a wooden skewer, press indentations all around the gold border (see photo).

8. Wrap the top of the clay piece around a skewer and press the clay onto the back to form a tunnel for the cord to go through. Remove the skewer by giving it a twist.

9. Bake the clay (see page 46).

10. Braid the three colored cords together. Thread the braided cord with the pendant between the two blue glass beads.

11. Attach the spring crimp (see page 44).

Versatile polymer clay is the secret behind the wonderful originality of this pendant necklace. A rubber stamp and magical, metallic powder helps you create a luminous dragonfly scene outlined in textured gold. Pale blue glass beads add to the look as does the colorful, braided cord suspending it all. Wear this on your next visit to the local art gallery.

MOKUME GANE CHOKER (BY MARIE SEGAL)

You'll need:
Clay: 1/4 block of Black, Ecru, Translucent, White, Gold, Leaf Green, Dusty Rose
Liquid Polymer Clay
Wooden skewer
2 gold beads (10mm)
Choker wire

1. Condition all colors of the clay (page 46).

2. Stack 1" x 2" sheets of Black, White, Gold, Leaf Green and Dusty Rose. Press the stack all around on the edges. Put the stack through the pasta machine on the thickest setting. Then put through one more time. Turn the stack over and with the blade, cut thin slices off of the stack. You will use only one slice for the pendant decoration.

3. Lay the slice of clay on a smooth surface. Press the rubber stamp into it firmly so that it cuts clear through to the surface. Do this in several places (see photo). Use a blade to remove it from the surface when you are ready to place it on the Black piece.

4. Follow the faux ivory instructions on page 47 to make the base of the pendant.

5. Cut the faux ivory to 3" high with sides sloping from 1 1/4" at top to 1 3/4" at bottom (see photo). Leave the bottom ragged just as it comes out of the pasta machine. Roll the top 1/2" of the ivory piece over a skewer and press into the back of the piece to form a tunnel for the wire to go through.

6. Run the Black clay through the pasta machine on a medium setting to form a smooth sheet. Cut a piece from this sheet 2" high with sides sloping from 1/2" at the top to 1" at the bottom (see photo). Attach this to the ivory piece using Liquid Polymer.

7. Attach the mokume gane slice to the Black piece using Liquid Polymer.

8. Bake the pendant (see baking instructions page 46).

9. Allow to cool. Then slide the pendant onto the choker with a gold bead on either side.

STAMPED PENDANT

You'll need:
Clay: 1/4 block of Black, Ecru, Translucent, White
Liquid Polymer Clay
Metallic Powders: True Blue, Misty Lavender, Blue Green
2 ivory beads (12mm)
Decorative rubber stamp
Choker wire

1. Condition all clay (see page 46).

2. Follow the faux ivory instructions on page 47 to use as the base of the pendant.

3. Cut the faux ivory sheet as shown in photo leaving one end ragged. Place it on a sheet of Black clay and cut around the Black about 1/8" larger.

4. Roll a ball of Black clay about 1". Press the rubber stamp onto the clay which will leave a design and flatten it. Dust this piece using a small paintbrush and the three colors of metallic powders. Blend the colors as you apply them.

5. Attach these three pieces together using Liquid Polymer.

6. Create two small round beads from the Black clay. Dust the beads with the same colors of powders. Pierce the beads using the needle tool (see page 46).

7. Bake all clay pieces. Allow to cool, then string the pendant on the choker with the beads on either side of the pendant (refer to photo).

What fun to show off your artistic talents with a small masterpiece nestled at the pulse point of your neck. With the help of polymer clay, you can make your own mini art canvas to wear on a wire choker. Polyclay forms the textured ivory and black backgrounds of both pendants shown here, as well as the colorful image designs at their centers. At top, the accompanying luminescent beads are made of polymer clay, while the bone beads are purchased. Gold metal beads accent the choker at right.

GENERAL SUPPLIES

Bead Board: When designing necklaces and bracelets, a bead board is an invaluable tool. The "U" shaped grooves allow you to arrange your beads without having them roll around. The board is marked in one-half inch and one inch increments which continue around the board. This allows you to determine the finished length of your piece. The instructions in this book refer to starting at the top of the board when arranging the beads. The "top" would be the length marked for the necklace or bracelet.

Flat-nosed (A) or Bent-Nosed Pliers (B): Both of these tools are used for bending and gripping wire. To avoid scratching your wire, use pliers that are smooth and not textured.

A

B

Round-nosed pliers (C): These pliers are used to form loops or curls.

C

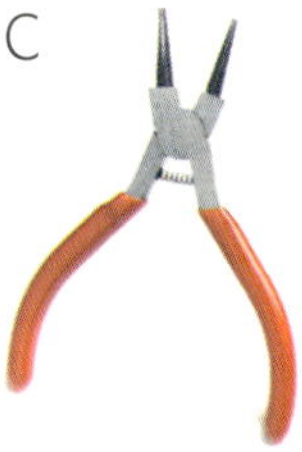

Needlenose pliers (D): These are also used for bending and gripping wire and are also useful for opening and closing jump rings.

D

Wire cutters (E): For cutting wire, eye pins and headpins.

E

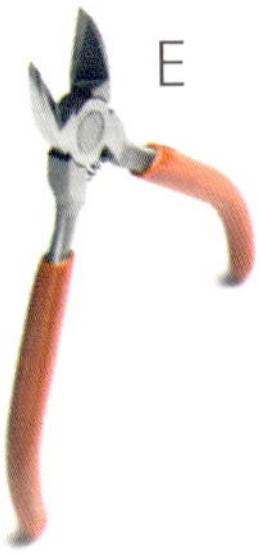

Crimping Pliers (F): To attach crimp beads. The pliers have notches that are used to fold and then press the crimp bead.

F

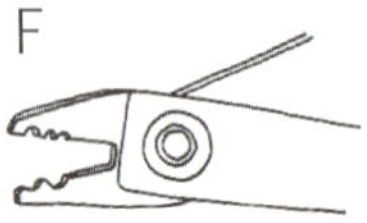

Beading Needles: There are several types and sizes of needles available. Consult your local craft or bead store for the correct one for your project.

Jewelry Glue: Used to reinforce knots and thread ends.

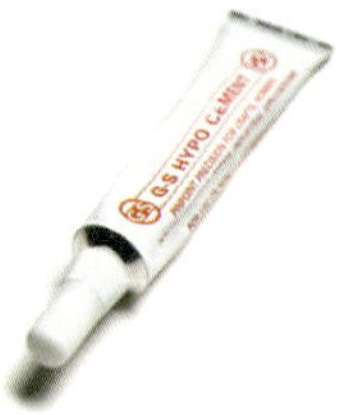

Stringing Materials

Beading thread, wire and cording is available in a variety of materials, sizes and colors. Choose the thread, wire or cord according to the bead size and weight.

The stringing materials listed below are just a few of the types available:

Thread

Woven thread: polyester thread is available in either 0.06mm or 0.04mm thicknesses. The thinner thread is a good choice for multi-strand necklaces.

Nylon thread: available in various thicknesses and colors. It works well when knotting is used in a jewelry project.

Wire

Beading wire: usually comes on a spool. There are many gauges of wire. The higher the number, the thinner the wire. Choose the wire depending on the project you're doing. For example, when constructing jump rings or eye pins you will need a thicker wire, for stringing beads, a thinner wire.

Coated Beading Wire: Soft Flex, Accu Flex and Beadalon comes in many sizes and colors. Soft Flex fine was used for many of the projects in this book. This wire is very flexible and easy to work with.

Elastic: Stretchy-style elastic is available in various colors and sizes. It is a popular material for making bracelets.

Cord

Leather cording: available in 1mm and 2mm thicknesses. It's a good material to use when hanging a single pendant. Leather-like cording gives a similar appearance.

Cotton cording: available in 1mm and 2mm and a wide variety of colors. This is an inexpensive alternative to leather cording. It can be used when you have knotting in your project.

Wax-coated cording: this cording comes in a wide assortment of colors and sizes. It holds its shape well and is a little easier to bead with.

FINDINGS

Eye pins: a straight piece of wire with a loop at one end.

Head pins: a straight piece of wire with a flat piece at the end.

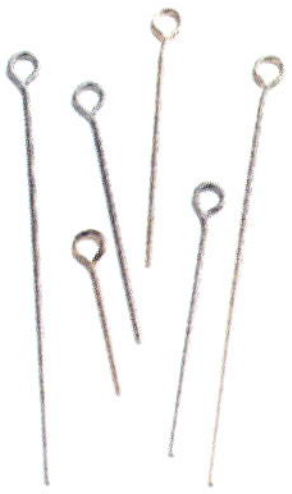

Crimp beads & tubes: These metal beads and tubes come in various sizes and are used to finish off a strand of beads before attaching a clasp.

Bead tips: These are used to finish necklaces that are strung on thread. The cup hides the knot, and the hook attaches to a jump ring or clasp.

Jump rings: Circles of wire that are available in various sizes. They're used to connect components such as clasps or beads. The rings are opened using hard nose pliers. Then closed again when the bead or clasp is added.

Clasps: Clasps are used to connect the ends of a piece of jewelry. They are available in a variety of styles and finishes. The clasp should coordinate with the beadwork.

barrel toggle spring crimp trigger claw 3 strand choker ball

End caps: These are used on the ends of multi-strand necklaces to create a finished look.

They are available in metal finishes, in cylindrical or conical shapes.

GENERAL INSTRUCTIONS

Threading and Wiring:

When determining the length of thread or wire to be cut, add 6 additional inches to the finished size of the necklace or bracelet.

Adding Bead Tips:

1. Attach a bead tip to the beginning of the jewelry piece by tying two overhand knots, one on the top of the other, at one end of the thread or cord.

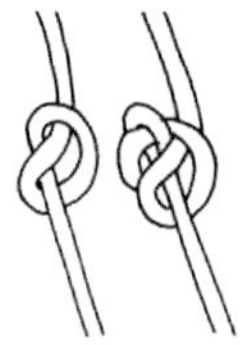

2. Thread the un-knotted end through the hole in the bead tip and slide it over the knot.

3. Cut off excess thread or cord and dab a small amount of glue on the knots.

4. Close the bead tip with the flat nose or needle nose pliers.

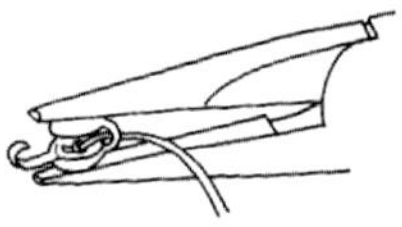

5. To attach the bead tip to the opposite end, thread the cord or thread through the hole in the bead tip. Tie an overhand knot and insert jewelry awl in the knot. Hold the cord and push the knot into the bead tip and pull tightly.

6. Remove the awl, trim excess thread, dab the knot with glue and close the bead tip.

Adding Crimp Beads & Tubes:

1. Thread one end of the beading wire through the crimp bead. Loop the wire back through the bead.

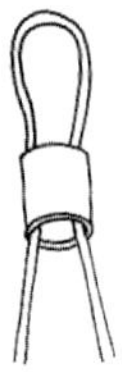

2. Position the bead in the notch of the pliers closest to you and squeeze. This forms a groove in the bead.

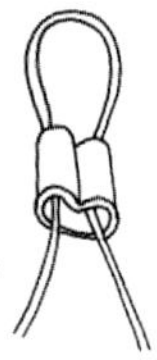

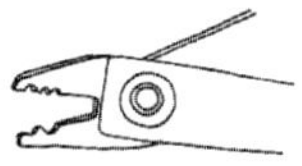

3. Position the bead in the second notch and squeeze. This will flatten the bead.

4. Cut excess wire with wire cutters leaving 1/4".

5. String beads on wire covering both pieces close to crimp bead.

6. After string is completed, thread on another crimp bead and position next to the last bead strung.

7. Loop the wire back through the crimp bead and last bead.

8. Hold the loop with round nose pliers and gently pull wire and the crimp bead next to the other beads.

9. Repeat the steps to close the crimp bead.

10. Cut off excess wire.

Adding End Caps:

1. After tying beaded strands together at one end with an overhand knot, cut off the loop of an eye pin. Use round nose pliers to form an open loop.

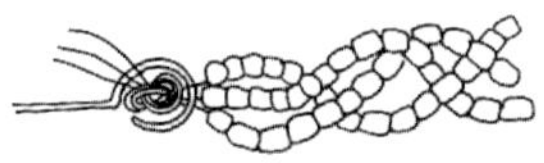

2. Hook the loop through the knot and then close. Thread the straight end of the pin through the hole in the end cap and pull the knot and beads into the cap.

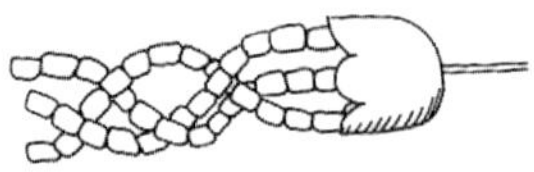

3. Trim excess wire leaving enough to form a loop for the clasp.

4. Repeat on the opposite end.

Adding the Clasp:

1. Clasps are designed with loops so they may be attached to bead tips, end caps or by crimping.

2. A spring crimp is attached to the cord by crimping the last ring. Spring crimps are attached with jump rings and toggles can be attached by crimping.

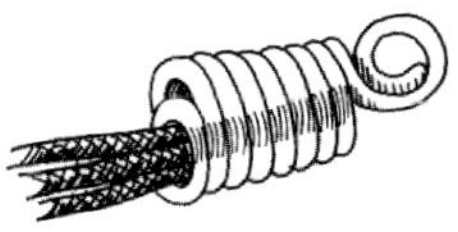

Traditional Knotting

An overhand knot is used when creating a necklace where a little space between beads is the look you want. Many jewelry makers prefer to knot between pearls and other high end beads. Knotting creates a nice draping effect to the necklace.

1. After the bead is threaded on the cord, tie a loose overhand knot.
2. Insert an awl into the knot.
3. Holding the cord in one hand, slide the knot down to the bead with the help of the awl.
4. Slip the awl out of the knot and tighten with your fingers. Diagram.

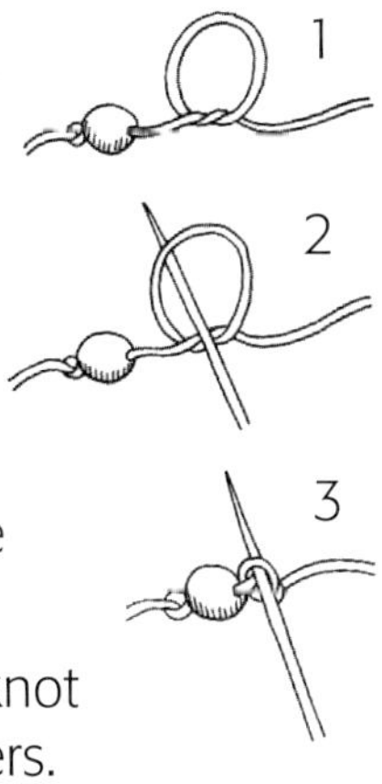

Square Knot

A square knot is one of the strongest knots. Follow diagrams 1 & 2 to tie one.

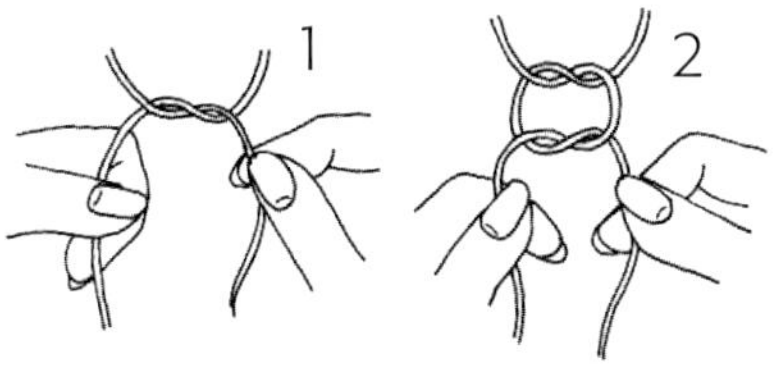

Forming a Loop

A loop is formed by bending the end of the wire around your round nose pliers.

Wrap Loops

The wrap technique creates a nice finished look to a number of projects:

1. After beading is completed, form a small loop with your round nose pliers.
2. While holding the loop with the pliers, use your fingers or needlenose pliers to wrap the remaining wire around the base of the loop and next to the last bead.

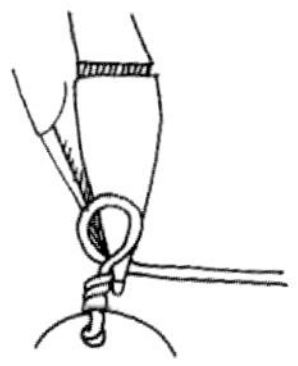

3. Wrap as many times as desired and trim excess wire.

POLYMER CLAY INSTRUCTIONS

Polymer clay

A smooth, soft, plastic clay-like substance. The clay can be formed into any shape and then baked into a durable object. There are several brands of clay available. We used Sculpey III and Premo! by Polyform Products. Both clays are available in a vast array of colors, plus translucent and can be mixed to achieve even more shades and hues.

YOU'LL NEED:

Cutting blade – also known as a slicing blade – for cutting clay.

Craft or utility knife – for precise cuts.

Needle tool – for piercing holes in beads. Wooden skewers or toothpicks can also be used.

Pasta Machine – to condition clay and make it into smooth sheets.

Roller – an acrylic clay roller for rolling sheets of clay when you don't have a pasta machine.

Brayer – used in place of the roller for rolling out smaller projects.

Conditioning the clay

By hand

When starting out you may wish to condition your clay by hand. Warm it first in your hands until it feels soft to the touch. Work with small pieces at a time. Roll the clay on your work surface and form a long log. Fold it in half, twist the two halves together and roll into a ball. Repeat this a number of times until the clay is soft and smooth. Place it on your work surface and roll it out using the roller or brayer.

Using a pasta machine

Cut off slices of the clay from the block. Place two or three slices side-by-side in the pasta machine and roll them through on the thickest setting.

Keep repeating this process, rolling the clay through on medium and then thin settings until the clay is a nice smooth sheet.

Making beads

Round beads – Roll between the palms of your hands until a round ball is formed.

Tube bead #1 – Roll out a log of clay. Cut along the log at desired intervals for bead. Pierce a hole using a needle tool.

Tube bead #2 – Make a 1" x 4" sheet of clay. Roll it around a wooden skewer. Smooth over the seam using your fingers. Roll the skewer on a flat surface to loosen the clay from the skewer. Cut into desired sections using the blade, then slide the bead off the skewer.

Experiment making other shapes such as squares, disks, donuts, etc.

Piercing holes in beads

Using the needle tool, drill a hole into the bead. After piercing all the way through, turn the bead around and drill the other way through the same hole. Be sure to make the holes large enough to accommodate the wire, thread, cord or jump rings you will be using in your finished piece.

Baking

Place the clay piece on a cookie sheet lined with parchment paper or piece of a brown paper bag. Place in the oven and turn it on to 200° and bake for 30 minutes. Then turn the oven to 275° and bake for 20 to 30 minutes more. Turn the oven off and let the pieces cool for about an hour before removing.

MOKUME GANE INSTRUCTIONS

(for pendant on page 36)

Supplies needed:

Clay: 2 oz. blocks of Ultramarine Blue, Lt. Blue Pearl, Translucent (Premo!), Purple (Sculpey III)

Silver Leaf
Paintbrush
Blade
Sculpey Glaze, gloss

1. Condition each color of clay. Make 5" x 2" sheets of each color and two of Translucent.

2. Layer the sheets in this order: Translucent, Light Blue Pearl, Purple, Ultramarine Blue.

3. Lay Translucent sheet on silver leaf and press it slightly. The leaf will stick to the clay. Trim excess leaf away from sheet.

4. Lay the Translucent sheet, leaf-side down on top of the stack.

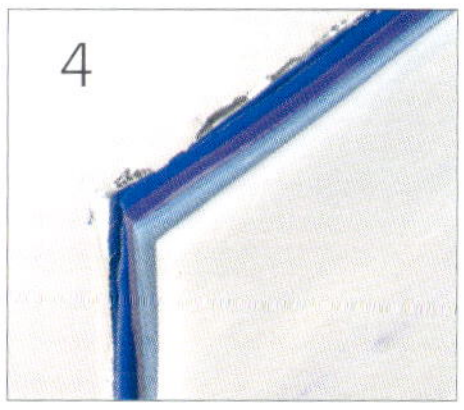

5. Cut the stack in half and stack one half on top of the other.

6. Pinch the stack to compress and flatten.

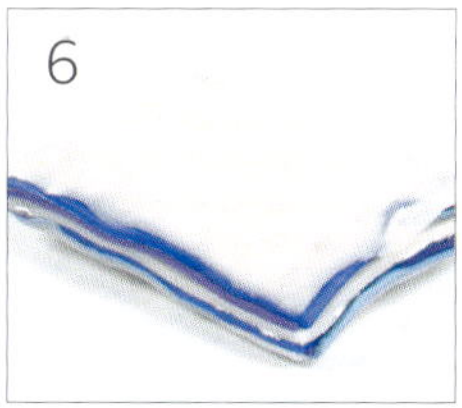

7. Cut in half and stack, pinch and flatten again.

8. Poke holes in the sheet using the end of a small paintbrush.

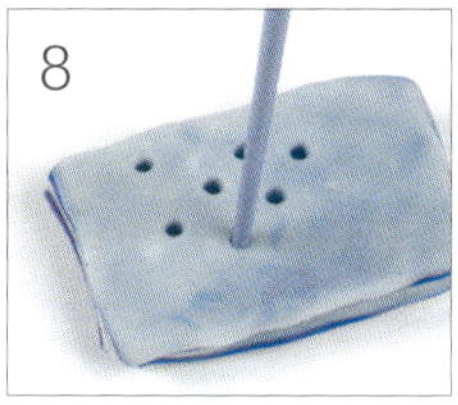

9. Stack, pinch and flatten again.

10. Cut in half. Place one stack on top of the other and pinch. Don't flatten.

11. Cut in half and stack again.

12. Use the blade to slice off thin slivers from the top of the stack.

13. Bake. Let cool, then apply glaze. Bake again for 15 minutes at 200°.

FAUX IVORY INSTRUCTIONS

Supplies needed:

Clay: 2 oz. blocks of Ecru, Translucent, White, Black (Premo!)

1. Condition all the clay.

2. Mix ½ block Ecru with ⅓ block White and roll through the pasta machine.

3. Roll the Translucent clay through the pasta machine.

4. Roll some of the remaining Ecru clay through the pasta machine.

5. Cut 2" x 2" sheets of the Ecru, Ecru/White mix, White and Translucent clay, and stack them in that order.

6. Cut the stack in half to 1" x 2". Stack these two halves and compress together. Flatten and stretch out to 3" x 2" sheet and cut in half. The stack will now be 1" x 2".

7. Repeat the above steps four more times, then cut the stack in half and stack one on top of the other, but do not flatten and stretch.

8. Slice off a ⅛" sheet from the stack using the blade.

9. Put the sheet into the pasta machine on the thickest setting (the lines should be going vertically).

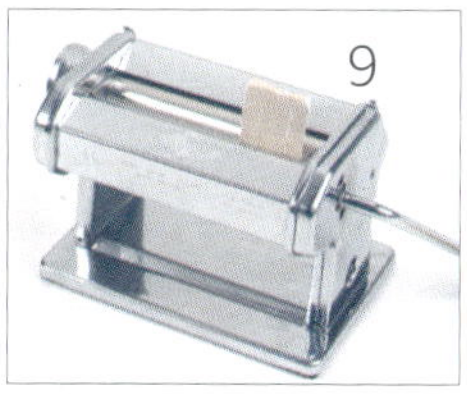

10. Turn this sheet a quarter turn and put through the pasta machine again on a medium setting.

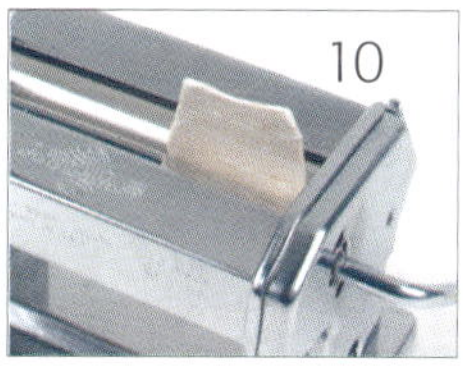

11. Put it through again on a thin setting. Then repeat on a thinner setting. Set aside.

SOURCES & CREDITS

Most of the supplies used in this book can be found in your local craft stores or craft departments of fabric stores, or bead specialty shops. If you can't find the item you're looking for, consult the following companies to find out where their products are sold:

CLAY SUPPLIES

The Clay Factory
P.O. Box 460598
Escondido, CA 92046
(800) 243-3466
www.clayfactoryinc.com

Polyform Products
1901 Estes Ave.
Elk Grove Village, IL 60007
www.sculpey.com
Sculpey and Premo Polymer Clay, Templates, Super Slicer, Liquid Sculpey, Sculpey Glazes

METALLIC POWDERS

Jacquard Products
Rupert, Gibbon & Spider, Inc.
P.O. Box 425
Healdsburg, CA 95448
Pearl Ex Powders

GOLD AND SILVER LEAF

Old World Art
1953 S. Lake Pl.
Ontario, CA 91761
www.oldworldart.com

Houston Art Inc.
10770 Moss Ridge Road
Houston, TX 77043
www.houstonart.com
Mona Lisa gold leafing products

BEADS

Mill Hill
Division of Gay Bowles Sales
3930 Enterprise Dr.
Janesville, WI 53546
www.millhill.com

Jewelry designs by Jerilyn Clements

Banar Designs Principals:
Barbara Finwall and Nancy Javier
Art Direction: Barbara Finwall
Editorial Direction: Nancy Javier
Writing: Susan Borsch

Photography: Stephen Whalen
Computer Graphic Design: Dana Allison
Project Direction: Jerilyn Clements
Designs by: Nancy Javier, Jerilyn Clements, Barbara Finwall & Marie Segal

Published by
LEISURE ARTS
LEISURE ARTS
5701 Ranch Drive
Little Rock, AR 72223

Produced by
BANAR DESIGNS
BANAR DESIGNS
P.O. Box 483
Fallbrook, CA 92088